# Claudine's Concert

Written by Virginia King
Illustrated by Bettina Guthridge

Sunday

Dear Diary,

We arrived at Aunt Claudine's today, and Toby asked if we could go camping. Aunt Claudine went pale. (We went camping last year – what a disaster!)

Aunt Claudine asked us to help her put on a concert instead. (I went pale. I was hoping for a nice quiet vacation.) She said we could help her make the costumes.

I was just thinking that helping might be fun when Aunt Claudine asked us to be _in_ the concert, too!

Toby says he'll be the star. I'm trying to get a sore throat!

Monday

Dear Diary,

This concert of Aunt Claudine's looks like it's going to be more like some crazy sort of variety show.

There are two ladies who are going to sing opera. There's a girl who is going to do gymnastics. (She says she can even walk on a tightrope!) And there's a magician.

Toby says he's going to juggle. (He keeps dropping oranges.) And Aunt Claudine is learning to play the violin.

I think I'll just watch.

Tuesday

Dear Diary,

Aunt Claudine spent all day writing. She's turned the concert into a play! It's called The Magic Spell. It's about a wicked magician who casts a spell on two opera singers to stop their singing.

A gymnast, a juggler and a violin player all try to break the spell, but they can't. Finally, a good fairy breaks the spell, so the ladies can sing again and make the world happy. (It's not a very good play, but it uses all the characters.)

"Who's playing the good fairy?" I asked. Aunt Claudine smiled.

Wednesday

Dear Diary,

Aunt Claudine thinks all girls want to be fairies.

I don't feel like a fairy. I feel like a pin-cushion! It took ages for Aunt Claudine to pin my costume – all those pointy pieces of pink material. (Aunt Claudine thinks all girls like pink, too.) I look like I'm wearing flower petals.

Toby spent all day dropping oranges. I'm sure my throat is beginning to feel sore!

Thursday

Dear Diary,

Today we made Toby's costume. I helped Aunt Claudine because Toby kept trying to juggle.

Toby's costume is even funnier than mine. He has a three-pointed hat and pointed slippers – and all the points have bells on them! I couldn't stop giggling, and I'm sure Toby dropped oranges on my head on purpose.

Aunt Claudine says he'll have to wear make-up, too – a big red circle on each cheek! (I'm going to take a photo of him to show his friends at school.)

Friday

Dear Diary,

Toby started painting the scenery today. I told Aunt Claudine that he can't paint, but she didn't listen.

I started to learn my lines. Aunt Claudine says I'm the most important person in the play! I have to say a lot of fancy words like, "Alas, these opera singers have been struck dumb by a wicked magician."

Then I have to sweep the air a lot with my magic wand. (It's just a paper star on a stick.) And then I say ... er ... oh no, I've forgotten!

Monday

Dear Diary,

The concert is only four days away and I don't know my lines yet. (I think I might still be getting a sore throat.)

Toby has finished painting the scenery. Yuk! He ran out of blue paint, so he painted the sky green! Aunt Claudine says it looks great. (She just doesn't want to hurt his feelings!)

Aunt Claudine put on her costume. I told her she looked like a princess.

Tuesday

Dear Diary,

We had a rehearsal today. Everything went wrong.

The magician's rabbit ran away. Toby wanted to juggle with eggs, but Aunt Claudine said to keep using oranges. He dropped five. Aunt Claudine's violin sounded like a wailing cat, and the gymnast knocked over the scenery. I forgot my lines, and the two opera singers argued about who was best.

After the rehearsal, we all had fruit juice and cake.

Wednesday

Dear Diary,

We had another rehearsal today.

This time the opera singers had an argument because they wore identical dresses. Someone sat on the magician's top hat. The sequins fell off the gymnast's costume. Toby tripped over an orange, and Aunt Claudine caught her sleeve on the violin bow.

But I was magnificent. My crown only slipped over my face a few times, and hardly at all when I was speaking.

Thursday

Dear Diary,

Aunt Claudine said that we should have a rest from rehearsals today. (The concert is tomorrow night!)

So I spent the day making beautiful programs. I wrote "The Magic Spell" in fancy letters, and I wrote "The Adventures of a Good Fairy" as well — so that people will know what the play's about. Then I wrote a list of all the actors' names. (I put my name at the top and Toby's at the bottom.)

Aunt Claudine made a lot of cookies to sell. I told her she'd better hide them from Toby.

Saturday

Dear Diary,

The concert was last night. Toby told Aunt Claudine that I had a sore throat, but I said that the show must go on!

Aunt Claudine was right - I was the most important person. I gave out all the programs, and I even sold two cookies. (Toby ate the rest.)

But the best part was my performance. Even when I forgot my lines, I just made them up or I did a little dance. The audience looked confused, but everyone clapped at the end. I was the star!

After the show Aunt Claudine suggested we go camping next year but I want to take acting classes instead.